D1436925

ABERDEEN

ABERDEEN CITY LIBRARY &
CULTURAL SERVICES

SUTTON PUBLISHING LIMITED

Sutton Publishing Limited
Phoenix Mill · Thrupp · Stroud
Gloucestershire · GL5 2BU

First published 1997

Copyright © Aberdeen City Council, 1997

British Library Cataloguing in Publication Data
A catalogue record for this book is available from the
British Library.

ISBN 0-7509-1375-4

Typeset in 10/12 Perpetua.
Typesetting and origination by
Sutton Publishing Limited.
Printed in Great Britain by
WBC Limited, Bridgend.

CONTENTS

Introduction   5

1. Working Lives   7

2. Childhood   39

3. Shopping   45

4. Getting About   55

5. At Play   67

6. Townscapes   77

7. Dressing Up   101

8. Something Special   111

Acknowledgements   128

Berry & Mackay, instrument makers on Marischal Street in the 1930s. Fascinated by the model ship and nautical paraphernalia, boys climb on to the window sill. Below the shop's name hangs the company's sign of the seaman with telescope.

INTRODUCTION

In 1875 George Washington Wilson wrote that most photographs 'deserve, after serving their temporary purpose, oblivion'. This is a pretty bleak assessment by Aberdeen's best-known photographer who was one of the most influential of the nineteenth century. But before we accept this judgement by Wilson we should remember that he was estimating the value of a photograph according to the standards of fine art.

Times and viewpoints have changed and we can no longer so easily dismiss photographs which stand outside the fine art tradition. Today the value of a photograph is not judged solely, or even principally, on some formal aesthetic standard. We now recognize that the worth of a photograph can reside in its documentary content, the fact that it can capture a scene or an event which has long since passed. But more than this, a photograph has that unique ability to bring us somehow emotionally closer to the flesh and blood of the past. Photographs have become key components of individual and collective memories.

Since the invention of photography in 1839 the sites and citizens of Aberdeen have been the subjects for countless thousands of photographers. In the earliest days George Washington Wilson carried his bulky wet-plate camera, with heavy glass negatives, developing tent and chemicals the length and breadth of the city. In the process he captured magnificent views of the architecture of Aberdeen and the hustle and bustle of city life. He showed how Union Street was at the heart of the expanding Victorian city. Originating at the Castlegate, an ancient place of civic and commercial life, the street stretched westward to the Denburn where in one leap it crossed the formidable gap and proceeded to the outskirts of the town. To the south lay the harbour which had been much improved by the engineering work of John Smeaton. As the nineteenth century progressed the harbour became an increasingly important part of the economic life of the city, handling imports from other parts of Britain and from overseas, and at the same time exporting agricultural products, textiles and granite to markets beyond the city. To the north, commercial activity thinned but the harbour provided access to the rural hinterland which fed Aberdeen.

As we stroll through the streets of nineteenth-century Aberdeen we become aware of how important the granite industry was to the city in particular and the north-east of Scotland in general. Most of the grand, and not so grand, buildings photographed in the last century were constructed of granite. A great deal of it came from Rubislaw Quarry on the edge of the city and many thousands of tons from outwith Aberdeen, most notably from Kemnay Quarries. The result was the Granite City, which on a bright sunny day sparkled like silver but which, in the cold and wet of deep winter, could look dour and deeply sombre. This architectural ambivalence was found not only in statements of civic pride and pomp such as the Town House of 1872, but also in the lofty tenements which went up later in the nineteenth century. Scattered throughout the city, particularly to the north, were many granite yards employing thousands of skilled men whose cutting, carving and polishing abilities were much sought after. Their legacy is to be found not only in architecture and civil engineering the length and breadth of Britain, but also in the thousands of granite memorial stones in cemeteries all over the country.

By 1900 photography had become easier. Roll film was invented in the 1880s and Kodak introduced its box camera with the motto, 'You Press The Button We Do The Rest'. This eventually opened the door to the amateur 'snaps' industry of today which has become such an important source of historical information. Just as photography was moving in a radically new direction, so industry in Aberdeen was changing; the introduction of steam trawling made the city one of the premier white-fish ports in the world for almost 100 years. Trawling not only introduced the bustle of the fish market to the harbour, but also gave an enormous boost to the shipbuilding industry. Aberdeen's shipyards already had a world-wide reputation for their sailing ships, especially those which boasted the 'Aberdeen Bow'. This design took advantage of customs regulations and gave increased speed, particularly useful to clipper ships which required speed and maximum cargo space. The advent of steam trawling gave men work on the boats, encouraged the expansion of processing at the quayside and stimulated the shipyards. All in all, it was of great importance to the city.

And so Victorian Aberdeen grew beyond the confines of its old centre. New tenements were going up all over Aberdeen, including across the River Dee at Torry. The working and lower middle classes were housed in buildings which were substantially better than earlier tenements and at times incorporated some very elegant features. Leisure within the city became increasingly important for all classes of society. The Art Gallery provided an alternative to public houses, a place where granite workers and others might learn the fundamentals of 'good taste'. Parks such as the Duthie Park allowed those weary from long hours at work to relax in pastoral surroundings, apparently well away from the noise and grime associated with city life. Of course, Aberdeen also had in its favour the fact that it nestled against the North Sea. A day at the seaside became a way of life. The beach was a place to play and relax, a place where citizens and visitors could forget the nearby shipyards and gas and chemical works. And there was the train. The railway from the south reached Aberdeen as early as 1850. By the mid-1850s a line had been pushed as far as Huntly, later to be extended to Inverness, and by 1866 Royal Deeside was open to railway traffic, taking visitors almost to the gates of Balmoral Castle. The combination of these services not only eased the movement of goods but at the same time made travel more convenient. Railway excursions to and from Aberdeen became part of the city's life.

These and many other features of Aberdeen's history are captured in the photographs in this book. They are drawn from the collections held by Aberdeen City Library and Cultural Services and form a significant resource in the history of the city. They give us a window on the past, introduce us to a city which Aberdonians of today can find familiar and yet which seems sufficiently distant and distinct to hint at different ways of life, different rhythms and different preoccupations. In most cases we do not know who the photographers were but we do know that by recording the sights of Aberdeen they have performed a most valuable service, allowing us to see where we have come from and hence helping us to know where we are today. Their work has not, as George Washington Wilson might have wished, been consigned to oblivion.

Aberdeen City Library & Cultural Services

WORKING LIVES

*A granite settmaker sitting in his 'Scathie', a hut
which could be turned for protection from wind and
rain, 1930s. Men such as this made the millions of
granite cassies which once paved the streets of Britain.
Settmaking was a skilled job and workers were paid
according to the weight of cassies they produced. It
was also hazardous, eye injuries being a particularly
serious problem. The widespread introduction of
coated roadstone materials killed off the craft of
settmaking.*

The best-known photographer of Victorian Aberdeen, George Washington Wilson, 1860s. He was trained as a painter of miniature portraits, but he recognized the potential of photography. From small beginnings he went on to become 'Photographer to the Queen' and a businessman of some wealth. His photographic works on St Swithin Street was an industrial enterprise which employed some 150 people and produced hundreds of thousands of images of Aberdeen and beyond.

G.W. Wilson's photographic works, St Swithin Street, 1880s. The female employees are printing directly from glass negatives, the sunlight acting on sensitized paper. In the event of rain, the mobile printing frames were wheeled indoors.

Rubislaw Quarry in 1884 was very different from the 480-ft hole left when the quarry closed in 1970. Granite from the quarry not only built much of Aberdeen, but also found its way all over the world in the shape of bridges, memorials, even paving setts.

Stonecutters at work in Rubislaw Quarry, 1890s. Behind them can be seen early hand-derricks for lifting the large granite blocks.

The interior of a granite works in the city where both traditional and pneumatic tools are being used. At the turn of the century Aberdeen had more than ninety granite merchants' and stonecutters' yards in operation, which exported more than 70,000 tons of granite.

The Masons' and Granitecutters' Union, 1888. Masons were members of a skilled and proud tradition and fought hard to protect their rights and privileges. In the early days of the union there were strict demarcations between those who worked on monumental work, those who were settmakers and those who tended polishing and other machines. As the trade was mechanized, so many struggles erupted to protect craft rights. Gradually, however, these were lost.

Masons working on unidentified architectural work at Charles McDonald's Froghall Granite Works, one of the largest granite works in the city, *c.* 1900. It is clear from the size of the granite blocks and pillars being worked upon that this was a project of some significance.

Carving the Lion for the War Memorial, 1920s. In the foreground is James Philip, one of the most skilled men in the granite trade. He is seen taking dimensions from the sculptor's plaster model. Behind him, with pneumatic tool, is George Cooper Clark working on the Kemnay granite from which the memorial was cut.

Skilled carver Thomas Pirie working with a pneumatic tool on the Cowdray coat of arms for Dunecht Estate. Pneumatic-powered carving tools were introduced to Aberdeen's granite trade in the 1880s, revolutionizing the cutting of monuments and ornate building work. These power tools were used to cut most of the draped urns and angels which grace many of Britain's cemeteries.

Mason James Philip uses a hand puncheon on the rough form of the Edward VII statue which now stands at the corner of Union Terrace and Union Street. Designed by sculptor Alfred Drury, this monument is cut from Kemnay granite. James Philip spent all his working life in the employ of Arthur Taylor of Jute Street and while there was responsible for carving a monument to the memory of those lost on the *Titanic* as well as numerous memorials to those who died in the First World War.

Building masons at a housing development on Queen's Road, near Hazlehead. For most of the nineteenth century and half of the twentieth century, granite was the stone most commonly used in Aberdeen buildings. From the humblest of tenements to grander houses in the city's west end it was the material of choice.

A Jenny Lind polishing machine being used in Charles McDonald's granite yard, Jute Street. The Jenny Lind took its nickname from the humming sound of polishing, said to be reminiscent of the famous Swedish singer's voice. Introduced from America in the 1880s, the machine was, and is, ideal for polishing small areas such as the faces of memorial stones.

Splitting granite by the plug-and-feather method, Rubislaw Quarry, 1960s. Despite the introduction of many sophisticated technologies into granite-working, this age-old method of splitting stone still finds a place in the industry.

Aberdeen's steam paddle tug, *Fairweather*, possibly on sea trials in the bay. Paddle steamers were highly manoeuvrable and as such were most useful for working in harbour areas. In the late 1880s many paddle steamers were converted to beam trawlers.

Looking across the River Dee from Torry, *c.* 1871. In the distance is the spire of the new Town House, clad in builders' scaffolding. The River Dee is in the process of being diverted to the course it follows today. The river previously ran farther north, parallel with the railway, towards the station at Guild Street. The dam in the right foreground was built to facilitate cutting of the new channel.

Hall's shipyard with workers and managers in front of partially built wooden ships, 1862. The figure standing directly beneath the bows of the ship on the right is William Hall, to his right stands his son Alexander, and next to him William's brother, James. Hall's shipyard was taken over by Hall Russell & Co. in 1957, which subsequently went into liquidation in 1991.

A graving dock for the repair of steamships was opened in 1885 at the east end of the Albert Basin, near the present-day Atlantic Wharf. Built of large concrete blocks with heavy metal gates, the dock was in use for almost forty years until superseded by a pontoon in 1913. The graving dock re-opened briefly during the First World War, but was eventually demolished in 1924.

Before the Commercial Quay fishmarket was opened in 1889, early trawlers landed their fish in the open air at Point Law.

The old and the new landing their catches at Aberdeen Fish Market: sail-powered Zulu skiffs alongside the recently introduced steam trawlers, *c.* 1900. Steam trawling revolutionized fishing and turned a craft practice into an industry.

A veritable shoal of dry cured fish at Allan & Dey Ltd, *c*. 1900. This company was one of the many that gave quayside support to the then rapidly expanding fishing industry in Aberdeen. Steam trawlers and line boats landed their catches at Aberdeen's market, the fish was processed and then carried by rail to markets in the south.

Women workers standing by a kiln preparing Finnan Haddocks, Allan & Dey Ltd, 1911. For a long time fish 'quines' such as these were the backbone of fish processing. Some followed the herring fleet as it chased and caught the shoals of fish round Britain's coastline while others worked in the more permanent fish houses in Torry.

The Upper Dock of the harbour with bucket dredger at work and a travelling steam crane on the quayside.

The once familiar sight of trawlers taking on coal at Point Law, *c.* 1950. The demise of steam power led to the eventual scrapping of this coal-handling plant. The trawler being coaled is A347, the *Viking Star*, built by Hall Russell & Co. in 1918.

Steam rock drill designed and manufactured by John M. Henderson & Co., 1880s. Used in conjunction with a portable steam boiler in local granite quarries, this was a major innovation which eventually made the slow, laborious hand-drilling method redundant.

Portable steam boiler manufactured by John M. Henderson & Co., 1880s. This was used in granite quarries to power rock drills. Established in 1866, Henderson's became one of the leading engineering firms in the city, supplying products such as cranes and cableways to all parts of the world. For economic reasons it relocated to Arbroath in 1985.

Skilled men in the pattern shop of John M. Henderson & Co., 1932. Like many other engineering yards in Aberdeen, Henderson's had its own foundry producing cast iron products of every description. Patternmakers made the complex wooden patterns (gear wheels, engine plates, etc.) from which moulds were made.

Women workers on parade down Union Street, 1940s. As part of the war effort these women had taken jobs in engineering with John M. Henderson & Co. and were encouraging others to do likewise. For brief periods (also 1914–18) women were allowed to enter the otherwise male-dominated engineering trade.

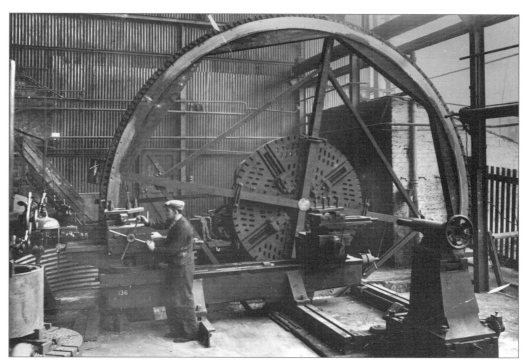

Large gap lathe facing the pivot sole for a derrick crane, John M. Henderson & Co., 1950s. The company established a world-wide reputation for its steam and electric derrick cranes. Examples of their products were to be found working in such places as quarries, on the building of dams in Egypt, the construction of the Forth Road Bridge and many other projects.

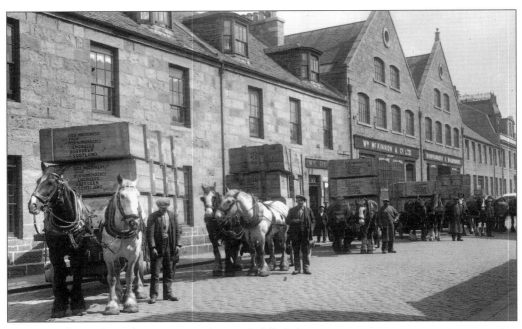

William Mckinnon's works, Spring Garden, with fully-laden carts preparing to carry rice-processing machinery on the first stage of a long journey to Siam. For almost two hundred years the company operated from these premises. In 1993 the business was transferred to Pittodrie Street. The Spring Garden site is now occupied by housing.

William Mckinnon & Co.'s machine shop 1914–18, with shell casing production well under way. Wartime demands gave a great boost to the engineering industry leading to the introduction of new machinery to meet the apparently insatiable demand for armaments.

Plantation device manufactured by William Mckinnon & Co., 1920s. This company established a world-wide reputation for the efficiency and reliability of its coffee, rice and cocoa processing machinery. Here workers in the company's works at Spring Garden demonstrate a simple plough-like piece of equipment for turning plantation products laid out to dry.

Barry, Henry & Co.'s works on West North Street, 1911. This company, which later became Barry, Henry & Cook, established a reputation for its mechanical handling equipment. It vanished from the city in the 1970s; the site of its former premises is now part of a supermarket complex.

The cast iron foundry of Barry, Henry & Co., showing moulders with moulding boxes and the ever present foundry sand, 1911. Foundry work was dirty, dusty, hazardous and skilled. Cast iron was the metal backbone of Britain's engineering strength in the nineteenth century, being used in the manufacture of steam engines, textile machinery, machine tools, decorative railings, etc.

'Barry's Bhoys', a proud group of engineers at Barry, Henry & Co., 1911. Seniority in engineering works was (and still is) often marked by dress codes; note the man with collar and tie (front row, fourth from the right), presumably a foreman or similar figure.

Dee Village was a self-contained hamlet standing at the foot of Crown Street. It grew up at the end of the eighteenth century to provide housing for the workers at the nearby pottery and brickworks in the Clayhills. The photographs show the village in 1898, the year before its demolition to make way for a new electricity station in Millburn Street.

Dee Village was demolished in 1899, and by 1 April 1901 the site had been completely cleared and the foundations were being laid for the new electricity station on Millburn Street.

By 1 August 1901 the building was well underway. Note the horse in the foreground, used for pulling the blocks to the required position.

By the beginning of July 1901 a start had been made on building the chimney which would eventually dominate the Millburn Street site.

The beginning of August 1901 saw the chimney reaching a third of its eventual height. By the end of December it was complete.

Corporation Electricity Showroom on Union Street, 1926, when electricity for domestic heating and lighting was beginning to challenge the dominance of gas. This was at a time when the Corporation ran both the gasworks and the electricity works.

The Corporation Electricity Works at the corner of College Street and Millburn Street with railway arches behind. This photograph was taken in 1926 when new steam turbines were being installed to meet the ever-increasing demand for electric power, in the days before the National Grid.

The water tower of the Northern Co-op's Dairy, Berryden, 1928. This well-known concrete landmark was demolished on 3 July 1994.

Staff and premises of the Northern Co-op's Dairy, Berryden. When opened in 1927 it was one of the largest and most modern dairies in Scotland.

Northern Co-op's site, Berryden, 1994. In the early 1990s the Co-op hit severe financial troubles. In an attempt to stave off bankruptcy it sold off various parts of its empire, including the bakery and the dairy. These sites were cleared to make way for new businesses. In the end, however, this was not enough to save the Northern Co-op and after some 132 years of trading the business went into liquidation.

Millbank meal and barley mills, Berryden, 1883. At one time this large urban mill employed ten millers. Its size is a good indication of the importance oats once had in the Scottish diet. The mill remained in production until the 1960s and was eventually cleared from the site in 1988 as part of the redevelopment of the Northern Co-op's premises.

Workers at Sandiland Chemical Works, between Cotton Street and Links Road. John Miller established his chemical business in 1848 and for generations 'stinky Miller's' was the source of well-known smells down at the beach.

Aberdeen School of Shorthand, Crown Street. In the early years of the twentieth century, office work became an important source of genteel employment for women. It is one of those rare examples where a previously male-dominated area of employment was overturned, giving birth to the archetypal female office worker.

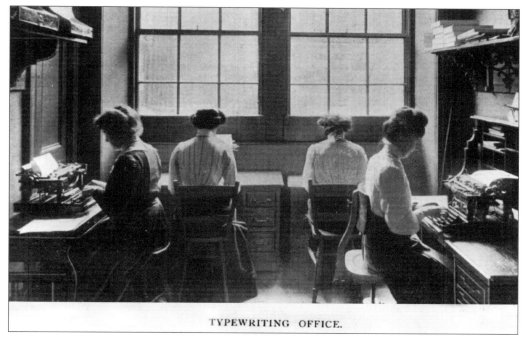

TYPEWRITING OFFICE.

TYPEWRITING CLASS ROOM.

PUPILS — SESSION 1909-10.

CHILDHOOD

*Sailor suits were a long-lasting, almost universal
fashion, arising from the Victorian obsession with
pretend uniforms. This boy was photographed in
about 1890.*

George Washington Wilson photographed his daughter Annie in 1864 wearing a crinoline style dress in imitation of adult fashions.

These boys in similar dark woollen embroidered dresses were photographed in this elaborate setting by George Washington Wilson in the late 1860s.

Children were often dressed in identical clothing, girls especially wearing elaborate dresses just like their mothers. This photograph, *c.* 1866, shows two small girls with tight-fitting crinoline skirts and fine leather gloves, with elaborate ringlet hairstyles.

Adams' photograph in the late 1890s is more relaxed, although the children still wear elaborate clothes.

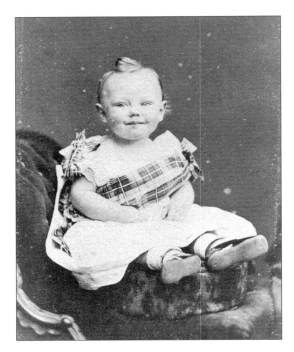

White embroidered dresses with tartan sashes were the height of fashion from 1850 to 1879, worn by girls and boys alike. Leather button ankle band shoes were a sign of babyhood also worn by both sexes. Occasionally a toy is featured, although it does not always shed light on whether the sitter is a boy or girl!

This Victorian primary class in one of the new School Board schools in the city is very attentive to the teacher's instructions. The exact location of the photograph is unknown, but the tiered and stepped classroom with its wrought iron and wooden desks was typical of the period and for many years to come.

A housewifery or domestic science class in one of the new School Board schools at the turn of the century. By the beginning of the twentieth century, the School Board was attempting to provide a more rounded education for girls. In 1904 they provided new facilities at the Girls' High School — not only for cookery and laundry work, but also for chemistry, physics, biology and art.

Boys from the Grammar School working in a garden plot on the south side of the school running down towards the Denburn.

Grammar School boys on nature study classes on the banks of the River Dee.

SHOPPING

*Window display at Alexander Auld's shop on
St Swithin Street.*

At the Sign of the Key, James Stephen, ironmonger, Broad Street, 1860s. A rather splendid example of a Victorian shop sign over a shop which sold everything from handcuffs to anvils, tin baths to keys.

Alexander Auld's grocery shop at the corner of St Swithin Street and Hartington Road, at a time when working in a grocer's business demanded many skills, such as preparing ham and bacon, blending teas and roasting coffee.

The Timmer Market in the 1890s was a thriving concern with stalls stretching the length of the Castlegate. The market continued late into the evening, selling everything from fruit to 'tattie chappers' and wooden toys.

The New Market, Aberdeen's first attempt at supermarket shopping, opened on 29 April 1842, gathering traders from all over the city under its roof – in one passageway alone there were fifty-four butcher's shops. Exactly forty years later, on 29 April 1882, the market was almost completely destroyed by fire. After it was rebuilt in 1883, only twenty-three butchers returned. The building was eventually demolished in 1970, after considerable local protest, and the site is now occupied by British Home Stores and Aberdeen Market.

Baker and assistants at the shop of James Milne, King Street, *c.* 1905.

The proprietor and staff of Robert Burr's haberdashers shop, 20–22 George Street, *c.* 1905. Robert Burr started in business in 1882 as Burr & Donald, drapers, at 38 George Street, moving to these premises in 1887 when Mr Donald retired.

From the 1920s to the mid-1950s, Wilburn's was one of the foremost grocers in Aberdeen, with branches throughout the city. The interior of the Hill Street shop in the 1930s is a reminder of the days when cake was sold by the slice, fancy cakes at five for 2d, and tea and sugar were weighed out from tin chests and large sacks on the balance scales.

In the 1930s, '50s and '70s Aberdeen Council photographed Union Street's shop frontages on a Sunday afternoon. This record gives us an invaluable insight into the look of the street, and the shop stocks, although many had their blinds pulled in earlier years. This image of Gordon's chemist shop comes from the 1950s series.

More images from this series of photographs, showing Guinea Gowns at the top end of the street, displaying a selection of everyday fashions, and Raffan's, at no. 42, further down the street, featuring reductions on all suits.

Shoppers queue for entry to Isaac Benzies' fifty-fifth anniversary sale in 1949. The store, based in George Street, took its name from its founder. It started as a baby linen business and developed into a store of four floors with restaurant and hairdressing salon.

Competing for the best sales bargains at Isaac Benzies. The store was one of the original 'one-stop shops' and a favourite with the Aberdeen public. It closed in 1986 having traded as Arnotts, part of the Fraser group, for many years.

Mascot Fashions boutique selling flares, hot pants and the mini in the late 1960s.

Officers from the City's Department of Weights and Measures checking the weights of products in a grocer's on King Street, *c.* 1969, before decimalization.

GETTING ABOUT

Aberdeen Suburban Tramways first introduced electric trams on the Deeside route in 1904. The fare from Mannofield to Bieldside, where the tram terminated, was 2d and remained so until 1918. The photograph shows car no. 5 at the Mannofield depot, with driver, George Cormack, in the middle of the group.

The Aberdeen to Inverness stage coach, *Defiance*, with travellers in fancy dress on an unidentified special occasion. As early as 1811 a coach was running all year round between Aberdeen and Inverness, but with the opening of the railway line to Inverness in the 1850s the days of coaching were numbered.

During the latter half of the nineteenth century, the Cluny coach was a familiar sight on the streets of Aberdeen. Originally running four days per week, by 1878 the coach made daily trips to and from Cluny. It departed its stance outside the Lemon Tree Bar in St Nicholas Street for the last time at 4 p.m. on Friday 31 August 1906.

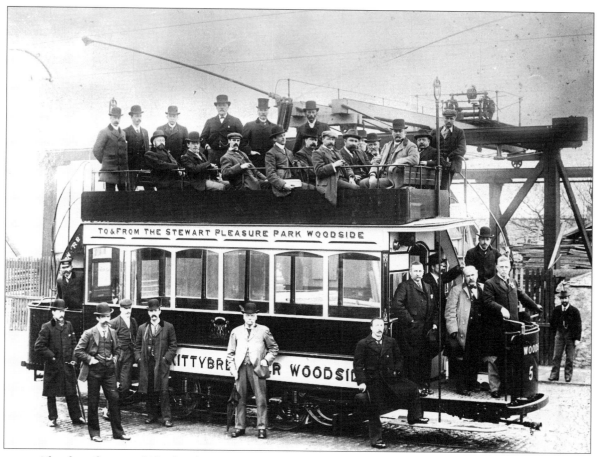

The electrification of Aberdeen's tramway system began in 1899, the Woodside route being modernized first. The tram in the photograph, with Lord Provost Fleming at the helm, took part in the inaugural procession.

The men who drove and collected the fares on the Woodside trams. The tram service to Woodside was originally part of Aberdeen District Tramways, the first horse-drawn tram travelling the route in 1880. In 1898 the service was taken over by Aberdeen Corporation Tramways.

Looking west up Union Street, *c*. 1950, with very few private cars on the road; buses and trams were still the principal means of transport. The older tram on the right travelling along Union Terrace contrasts with the newer 'streamlined' model in the foreground.

By the beginning of the 1860s two separate railway companies operated into Aberdeen – the Scottish North Eastern Railway from the south with its station at Guild Street, and the Great North of Scotland Railway Co. with stations at Kittybrewster and Waterloo. The Denburn Valley Junction Railway Scheme – to link up the lines from Kittybrewster to Guild Street – involved enclosing the Denburn in a culvert before the railway line could be laid. The photograph shows the commencement of work on the stretch adjoining what is now Union Terrace Gardens.

Aberdeen Joint station under re-construction, October 1913.

Guild Street station from the south in the 1870s. On the extreme right can be seen the original oak and lead steeple of St Nicholas' Church as it was before the east church was destroyed by the fire of 1874.

In 1896, the Great North of Scotland Railway Company, which operated the lines from Aberdeen to Inverness and Deeside, introduced a new range of six-wheel carriages. These offered passengers new comforts such as electric lighting, lavatories and corridor coaches.

Interior of Aberdeen Joint station in 1912 showing Knowles' confectioner's stall and the old metal advertising signs.

The magnificent old booking office at Aberdeen railway station, 1970s. This large wooden structure was swept away when the station was modernized by British Rail.

Aberdeen Corporation Gas Works' locomotive pulling wagons of coal from Trinity Quay to the gasworks on Cotton Street, 1930s.

An early example of a private car in Aberdeen, *c.* 1901. The family group at Seafield House is that of John Harper, engineer; he is the bearded figure in the front of the car.

City officials inspect a newly acquired vehicle at the Fire Brigade's King Street premises.

A beautifully decorated Knowles & Sons lorry parked in Marine Terrace. Coachwork for this vehicle was by J. & J. Ingram of Hutcheon Street. Ingram's work had originally been with horse- and hand-drawn carts. The coachbuilding and cartwright skills of the company were easily turned to meet the requirements of building and decorating the coachwork of motor lorries.

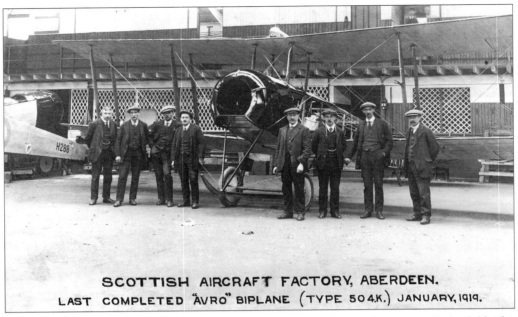

January 1919 and the last 'Avro' biplane is completed at the Scottish Aircraft Factory at Forbesfield. This was one of the final reminders of war production in the city.

A very young Eric Gandar Dower in the cockpit of a Blondeau Hewlet Farman biplane, 1913. Eric Gandar Dower was the man who, before 1939, established Aberdeen Airways and developed Dyce Airport, pioneering flights to and from the Northern Isles and Norway.

AT PLAY

*Young boy dressed in full highland dress, c. 1890.
The patent pumps and pose adopted for the
photograph suggest that he was a regular competitor
at highland dancing competitions — possibly even a
prize winner.*

Bankhead station is crowded by eager families waiting for the train to take them into the countryside for the Stoneywood church picnic, *c.* 1900. In spite of the excitement, the Stoneywood Sunday School superintendent, William Watson, and teacher, John McHardy, are keeping the crowds in order as they wait to board the train.

Stoneywood Church picnic at Bankhead station.

As they do today, many of Aberdeen's citizens headed up Deeside in summertime for a relaxing day out. This picnic group was photographed in the late 1890s.

THE BATHING BEACH, ABERDEEN.   4045   G.W.W.

Aberdeen beach in the 1880s, featuring the bathing machines which served to protect the modesty of Victorian bathers. Huts on wheels, they were pulled down to the water's edge by horses, allowing the bather to step straight from the privacy of the changing room into the water.

This photograph of Aberdeen beach shows, on the skyline, the Beach Bathing Station in all its Victorian splendour. It was the epitome of seaside luxury, having refreshment rooms, ladies' and gentlemen's retiring rooms and private baths. The Beach Baths as it became known closed on 11 July 1972.

Newhills tennis court, *c.* 1900. Lawn tennis was introduced into Britain in the early 1870s, and by the end of the 1880s tennis courts and clubs had sprung up throughout the north-east of Scotland. The long, elegant skirts of the ladies, while looking highly decorative, must have ensured a rather sedate game.

Cricket team, *c.* 1891, with Dr Andrew Hunter seated centre.

Aberdeen Postal Band outside Head Post Office, Crown Street, *c.* 1910. Designed by W.T. Oldrieve in baronial style, the General Post Office building was opened in 1907. Ninety years later its days as a post office building came to an end.

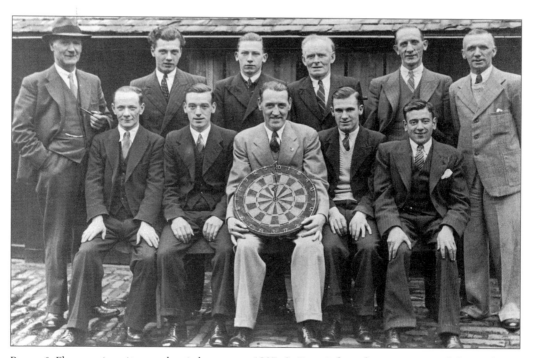

Bower & Florence (granite merchant) darts team, 1937–8. From informal games organized during dinner breaks, employees and management progressed to renting a room in which they could play darts, whist, dominoes, etc. Back row, left to right: J. McLaren, senior partner in the firm; A. Wisely, mason; E. Barneton, apprentice blacksmith; W. McKenzie, labourer; T. Barneton, blacksmith; Charlie the craneman. Front row: first two not identified; A. Niven, hand polisher; A. McLeod, mason; and G. Elphinstone, sawman.

The members of Trinity Cycling Club on a day out to Dunecht, west of Aberdeen, in 1898. The club was instituted in May 1897 and had an active programme, cycling to destinations such as Stonehaven, Crathes and Braes of Gight. Unlike the men, whose costume was suited to cycling, the women wore tight-fitting boned bodices and ankle-length skirts.

On stage with younger members of Miss Hendry's Dancing Class.

Group photograph of Miss Hendry's Dancing Class. Jeannie Hendry (extreme right) taught dancing and drama at her classes on Albyn Place for many years, culminating annually in a staged production at His Majesty's Theatre.

Donald Dinnie (1837–1916), the famous
Deeside athlete, wearing his full complement
of medals from Scottish Highland Games.
Some of the many medals won during his
sporting career are now in the collections of
Aberdeen Art Gallery & Museums.

The Dinnie medals and belt displayed in the Criterion Bar on Guild Street, 1944. Standing alongside is the
celebrated John Frost, licence-holder of the Criterion from 1923 to 1963. The Dinnie medals hung on the
walls of the bar until he retired.

TOWNSCAPES

Like many of the city's public buildings, the Town House was decorated for the celebration of Queen Victoria's golden jubilee on 21 June 1887. The Municipal Buildings, completed in 1874, incorporated the old Tollbooth; its seventeenth-century tower can be seen on the right.

Broad Street at its junction with Union Street was widened in 1867, shortly after this photograph was taken. The buildings on the right were demolished to make way for the construction of the Town House. The three top-hatted men standing in the middle of the street were prominent citizens of the time – Baillie George Ross, owner of a haberdashery on Broad Street; William Forsyth, editor of the *Aberdeen Journal*; and George Jamieson, Lord Provost of the city from 1874 to 1880.

The Royal Athenaeum was designed in 1818 – as the Union Buildings – to replace the earlier structures swept away in the construction of Union Street at the beginning of the nineteenth century. Originally a reading room, the Athenaeum was bought in 1881 by James Hay, becoming the Royal Athenaeum Hotel and Restaurant – better known to generations of Aberdonians as 'Jimmy Hay's'.

The Castlehill barracks, built in 1794 to accommodate visiting troops of soldiers, soon became the home base for the Gordon Highlanders. When the regiment moved to the Bridge of Don in 1935, the barracks were turned into flats, finally being demolished in 1965 to make way for a housing development.

The Market Cross was erected at the west end of the Castlegate, opposite the Town House, in 1686. It was moved to its present position in 1842. This photograph, from the last decade of the nineteenth century, shows it surrounded by iron railings which disappeared, like so many others, for the war effort in the 1940s.

The south side of the Castlegate in the 1930s featured the dilapidated remains of the twin-gabled sixteenth-century building known as Rolland's Lodging. Once the town house of the powerful Rolland family of Disblair in Newmachar, it was demolished in 1935. The site is now occupied by Voluntary Service, Aberdeen.

Exchequer Row, *c.* 1890. This old house was known as 'The Exchequer' and was believed to stand on the site of the royal exchequer which gave the street its name. Note the fish hake beside the door and the dovecot high on the wall. The house disappeared in the clearance scheme of 1895.

This old building in the Shiprow, opposite its junction with Shore Brae, was demolished for the building of Trinity Congregational Church in 1877. The church itself is now part of the city's Maritime Museum.

The house in the foreground, occupied by John Buchan, baker, was the last of the medieval houses in the Green; it was almost 300 years old when it was demolished in 1914. Aberdonians will remember with affection the golden teapot of John Adams and the wonderful smell of freshly roasted coffee which wafted out of the shop.

Until the beginning of the eighteenth century, Aberdeen's water supply came from the loch, burns and the ancient city wells — supplemented in times of drought by licensed water carriers. The first piped water was brought into the city in 1706 from springs at Carden's Haugh to a well, now affectionately known as 'The Mannie', in the Castlegate. In 1852 'The Mannie' was moved to the Green (see photograph above), returning to its rightful place in the Castlegate in 1972.

On 29 August 1884 the streets of Aberdeen were decorated for the visit of the Prince and Princess of Wales – the future King Edward VII and Queen Alexandra. The New Market, which had re-opened the previous year after a disastrous fire, won prizes for its decoration. The building was designed by Archibald Simpson with an extremely impressive façade on to Market Street.

Looking down Blairton Lane from Broad
Street, 1927. Blairton Lane, named after Lord
Blairton of Belhelvie, was swept away with the
clearance of the Guestrow after 1945.

The College Gateway, flanked by Ogston's Court and the College Gate Clothing Company, led from
Broad Street through to Marischal College and old Greyfriars church. The panel above the gateway shows
the coat of arms of George, 5th Earl Marischal, founder of Marischal College. All of these buildings were
swept away at the beginning of the twentieth century to make way for the granite façade of Marischal
College and the new Greyfriars church.

Provost Skene's House, now a period house and museum, in the late 1940s – the sole survivor of a slum clearance programme. This view from Broad Street is now obscured by modern buildings.

The opening ceremony of Provost Skene's House as a museum in 1953, after a long-running campaign to save the building from demolition. Extensive restoration work was carried out before the building could be opened by Her Majesty the Queen Mother.

A view of the Guestrow, 1927. Known locally as the 'Gush', the Guestrow was a notoriously rough part of the city. A large part of the area was cleared to make way for the 'modern' concrete and glass structure of St Nicholas House.

Thornton Court in the Guestrow. This scene seems more reminiscent of the Victorian era than the 1920s when it was photographed.

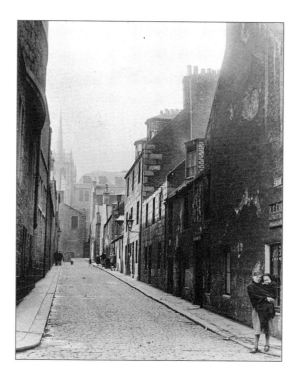

Looking up Shoe Lane towards Marischal
College, 1927. This lane takes its name from
the shoemaker craft of the Incorporated Trades
which laid it out with lamps in the eighteenth
century.

Looking up the Upperkirkgate towards Marischal College with St Nicholas Street off to the right and
George Street to the left. This street layout is now a memory: most of it was swept away with the building
of covered shopping centres in the 1980s.

Mars Castle stood on the east side of the
Gallowgate, almost opposite Innes Street and
Young Street, both of which disappeared with
the building of Aberdeen College. It was
reputed to date from the sixteenth century, but
by 1897 its condition had deteriorated so badly
that the Town Council ordered its demolition.

Looking down the Gallowgate with the sign of the Blue Lamp pub on the right, 1920s.

Before and after: the corner of Gaelic Lane and Belmont Street. In 1898 local printer G.W. Fraser took occupation of the new premises at the corner, having previously worked from the building seen in the earlier photograph.

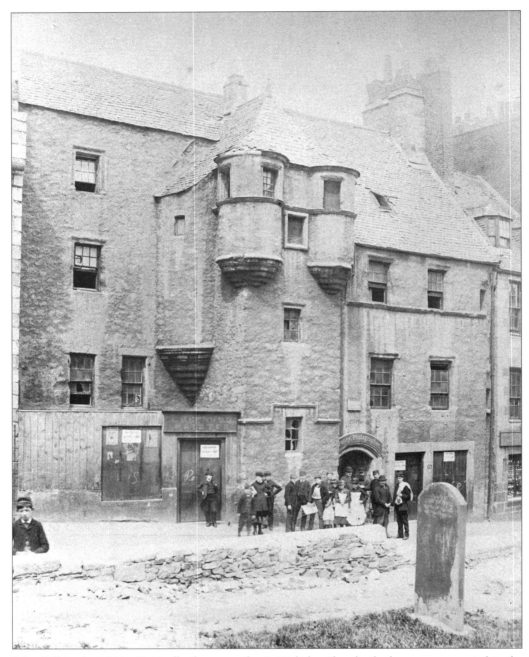

Schoolhill in the 1880s. Originally the manse for St Nicholas Church, the house was occupied in the 1620s by George Jamesone, the celebrated seventeenth-century portrait painter. The building was demolished in 1886, by which time it had become a lodging house.

Front and back views of 61 Schoolhill, *c.* 1970, before conversion to the James Dun's House Museum. The house was built in the 1760s for James Dun, one-time master and rector of the Grammar School. The Grammar moved from Schoolhill to its present site on Skene Street in the 1860s.

Views of the junction of Schoolhill and Blackfriar's Street, showing the Art Gallery to the right, before the addition of Cowdray Hall and the War Memorial. Lower photograph shows the Schoolhill façade of the Art Gallery.

Uniformed staff at the Art Gallery, *c.* 1905. The Art Gallery opened its doors to the public in 1884. Designed by architect, A. Marshall Mackenzie, the building incorporates red granite from Corrennie Quarry and the silver-grey granite of Kemnay. In 1905 the Sculpture Court was added.

Construction of the War Memorial and Cowdray Hall. The Memorial was officially dedicated in 1925. As in the older, adjacent Art Gallery, granites from quarries at Kemnay and Corrennie were used in the building.

In June 1902 the Public Library, along with many other civic buildings, was decorated for the forthcoming coronation of King Edward VII and Queen Alexandra. The photograph shows the original building, opened in 1892.

On 5 April 1892 Aberdeen Public Library opened its new building in Rosemount Viaduct with a complement of twelve staff, including a bookbinder and janitor. Eleven of the staff appear in this photograph, the absentee being the librarian, Alexander Robertson.

School visits started in the Central Library in 1945. Children from city schools were shown round all the departments of the library before answering a few simple questions on what they had seen.

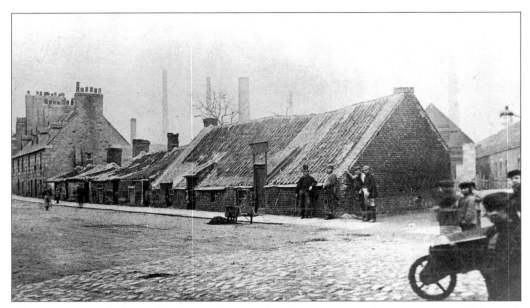

Gilcomston Steps which ran from Skene Square to Spa Street was once the home of many of the city's weavers. By 1866, when this photograph was taken, the houses had become so dilapidated that they earned the nickname, 'Rotten Holes'. This early slum disappeared in 1866 with the construction of the Denburn Valley Railway.

The Hardweird, pictured in about 1900, ran from Jack's Brae to Skene Row, and was fairly typical of the streets in this area of the city. In 1934 the Town Council designated it a slum clearance area and the houses were demolished.

Leadside Road, in the heart of Gilcomston, took its name from the mill lade which ran as an open stream from Gilcomston Dam to the town's grain mill on Flourmill Brae. This photograph, *c.* 1895, shows some of the earliest granite-built tenements in the city.

Building work underway at the corner of
Bridge Place and Bridge Street. The derrick
crane was manufactured by J.M. Henderson &
Co. of Aberdeen.

Dry privy in King Street, 1950s. Right up until the late 1960s the typical tenement flat in Aberdeen had
no bathroom and the toilet (if you were fortunate) was on the half-landing – at worst it was out in the
'backie'. Flush toilets were the norm, but as late as the 1950s, as this photograph shows, the dry privy
was still to be found in the city.

A peaceful, almost rural scene in Desswood Place in the 1890s. The street was named after Alexander Davidson of Desswood who was chairman of the Aberdeen Land Association, owners of the property on which the street was built.

A 1930s scene reminiscent of a small market town with pigs 'foraging' on Regent Quay, probably before being loaded on board a coastal trader for markets in the south.

VICTORIA BRIDGE ABERDEEN.   11569   J.V.

Victoria Bridge was opened on 2 July 1881, linking the city of Aberdeen with the neighbouring village of Torry on the south bank of the River Dee. Before the building of the bridge, the communities' main connection was by ferry boat. On 5 April 1876 the ferry, badly overloaded with passengers on a public holiday, sank with the loss of thirty-two lives. Public outrage at the disaster was largely responsible for the speedy construction of the bridge.

DRESSING UP

*Two sisters wearing the fashionable dress of 1873.
The dress bodices are long and tight with an apron-
like double skirt pulled and draped over a bustle.*

A fashionable couple photographed in the mid-1870s. Her hair is pulled back severely over her ears and temples and draped in a profusion of ringlets, accentuated by her small hat. She also follows the fashion of the day with her short velvet jacket and double bustle skirt. He wears a short frock coat with deep lapels and narrow bow tie.

An older couple photographed in about 1883, wearing outdoor clothes in a slightly 'out of fashion' style.

A G. & W. Morgan studio portrait of two
fashionable young ladies in outdoor dress,
c. 1880. Both wear tight-fitting costumes
elaborately trimmed with lace, ribbons and
jewellery.

Cabinet prints were popular from the 1880s
onwards, families often exchanging them for
albums at Christmas. This studio setting dates
from the late 1890s; the girls' looser-fitting
velvet dresses show the influence of the dress
reform movement.

An informal portrait of a family gathered around the front door of a granite cottage, typical of middle-class Aberdeen.

The daughter creates a fashionable silhouette for 1903 with her slim waist and large hat, in contrast to her more dowdy parents, in this studio photograph taken at The American Studio's Schoolhill premises.

A 'works' staff photograph taken on the steps of Union Terrace Gardens, *c.* 1906. The older women wear their best working clothes – a smart blouse and skirt – and all have fashionable bouffant hairstyles without fringes. The younger girls, some in their early teens, wear three-quarter length skirts with coloured, sometimes lace-trimmed blouses, dark stockings and button boots. The men, the proprietor and his managers, wear dark suits and cutaway frock coats.

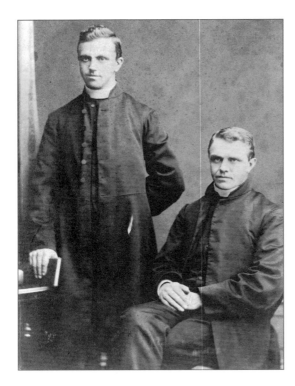

Two unidentified clergymen, thought to be graduates of Aberdeen University's Divinity Faculty.

Medics of Aberdeen University's Medical Faculty after their graduation in 1891. All wear evening dress with wing-collar shirts and bow ties.

A telegraph boy in a studio setting, *c.* 1900. Our collection contains a number of portraits taken with the sitter in uniform, either military uniform or that of civilian occupations and organizations.

Guide captain, May 1939.

Soldier in full dress uniform possibly of the Gordon Highlanders, 1899–1900, in Pietermaritzburg, Natal, South Africa during the Boer War. The card was sent home to a loved one in Aberdeen as a memento.

An unidentified soldier dressed in what is thought to be the uniform of the Aberdeenshire Volunteers, *c.* 1890. The Volunteers assisted in policing the city before the establishment of a professional police force.

There are fewer portraits of men in our collection than women. Many were taken in uniform, such as this portrait of Alex Battisby taken before departing for service in the First World War.

Portrait of a young man taken with his wife or fiancée, *c.* 1916, before his departure to join the forces in the First World War.

The Mortimer family pose for a group photograph shortly before the wedding of Elizabeth (middle, back row) in 1900.

SOMETHING SPECIAL

Studio portrait of Mr and Mrs Martin taken shortly after their marriage in 1904.

Two Aberdeen brides of the 1890s, wearing magnificent dresses of the finest quality ivory silk.

An Aberdeen couple at the time of their house wedding in the city's Baker Street, 1912. For reasons of economy, many chose to be married in their own homes, or reception rooms, which was allowed under Scottish law, rather than having a full church wedding.

Mr and Mrs Watt were married in the Gondolier Rooms in Silver Street on 8 June 1923. She wears a short straight dress gathered on the hips and a veil low on her brow. After the wedding Mrs Watt removed the beadwork trimmings, which were subsequently donated to Aberdeen Art Gallery & Museums' collections, and dyed her dress to wear on social occasions. Her husband wears a dinner suit and wing collar.

The wedding of Christina Moir and George Stephens took place in the Palace Hotel, 3 August 1927. This relaxed pose shows clearly the stylish short dresses and 'Louis heel' shoes worn by the bride and her attendants.

The wedding group of Andrew Craig and Mary Wood, 1909, illustrates a simpler style of dress. The bride (centre) has chosen a 'tailor-made' suit which she would be able to wear again for best and Sundays.

An informal portrait of Margaret Battisby and her sister in the back garden before Margaret's wedding.

Margaret Battisby married Lewis Hay on 14 July 1922 in Aberdeen; she wore a fashionably simple cut silk satin dress with simple orange blossom head-dress and veil clamped low on the forehead.

The west gate of the Duthie Park decorated for
the park's opening in 1883.

The Duthie Park was gifted to the citizens of Aberdeen by Miss Elizabeth Crombie Duthie, as a lasting
memorial to her brother and uncle. It was officially opened on 27 September 1883, the ceremony being
performed by Princess Beatrice, the youngest daughter of Queen Victoria. The day was declared a public
holiday in the city, and, despite the rain, crowds lined the route of the procession taking the Princess and
Miss Duthie to the ceremony.

Podium at the opening of the Duthie Park, 1883. The celebrations were somewhat dampened by heavy rain.

A triumphal arch straddles Broad Street, erected to welcome King Edward VII to Aberdeen in 1906 to open the extensions to Marischal College.

For four days in September 1906 Aberdeen celebrated the quatercentenary of its University. The highlight of the occasion was the inauguration of the new buildings at Marischal College by King Edward VII and Queen Alexandra. The King arrived at Holburn Street station on 27 September and travelled in procession through the city watched by over 200,000 people.

On the Broad Hill, 29 August 1912, and the first monoplane to land in Aberdeen.

Aberdeen Red Cross transport personnel and wagons assembled in the courtyard of Robert Gordon's College in 1917 prior to departure for the French front. This block of buildings was opened in 1912 as a new training centre for teachers; today it is part of the Robert Gordon University.

The Ailing Children's Camp on Scotstoun Moor provided holidays for children from deprived homes in the city, in need of good food and fresh air. All the food, clothing and fuel was donated and the money to run and extend the camp was raised locally.

The laying of the foundation stone for the King George VI Bridge over the River Dee took place on 15 September 1938, with Lord Provost Edward Watt officiating. A 'time capsule' containing council minutes, local newspapers, and coins was laid in the south pier of the bridge.

Launch of the trawler *Sir William Hardy*, Hall Russell shipyard, 1955. After twenty-three years' service as a fishery research vessel the *Sir William Hardy* was taken over by Greenpeace, renamed the *Rainbow Warrior*, and became part of the organization's militant struggle against environmental pollution. In a campaign against French nuclear tests, the *Rainbow Warrior* was targeted by French security services and sunk in its berth in Auckland, New Zealand. Not only was the ship sunk, but a member of the crew lost his life.

On 16 August 1884 over 10,000 men from more than thirty different trades paraded through the streets of Aberdeen to a demonstration on the Links. The 'Grand Old Man' of the banner was William Gladstone, who had introduced a bill to extend the vote to over 2,000,000 people. The House of Lords opposed the bill, an action which lead to popular demonstrations throughout the country in support of Gladstone.

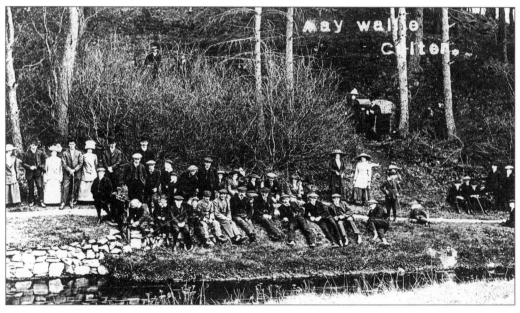

May Wallie, early 1900s. The May Wallie was situated on the banks of the Leucher Burn to the north of Peterculter. Like many wells and springs, the water of the May Wallie was believed to bring good health. For many years, May-day morning, or the first Sunday in May, saw a procession winding its way to the well to drink the iron-tasting water and perhaps make a wish.

The statue of Robert Burns in Union Terrace was unveiled in September 1892 by Professor Masson of Edinburgh University before a crowd of almost 7,000. Designed by Henry Bain Smith, the statue was cast at Moore's of Thames Ditton.

Following the tradition of centuries, the proclamation of King George VI's accession to the throne was read at the Market Cross on 14 December 1936.

The year is 1884 and clergymen gather in Aberdeen to celebrate the centenary of the consecration of Samuel Seabury as the first American Episcopal Church bishop. This momentous event of 1784 took place in the house of Bishop John Skinner of Aberdeen and marked the beginning of an independent church in the recently founded USA.

Bonfire, Brimmond Hill, 1935, celebrating the Silver Jubilee of George V and Queen Mary.

ACKNOWLEDGEMENTS

We would like to thank Allan & Dey Ltd and John M. Henderson & Co. for permission to reproduce the photographs on pp. 19–23. At the same time we welcome the chance to thank those many people who over the years have donated photographs to Aberdeen City Library and Cultural Services. The resource that they have helped to build is an invaluable record of the city's past. Without their generosity this publication would not be possible.